Awesome Animals

Lynn Huggins-Cooper

Activities by Tracey E. Dils

QEB

QEB Publishing

Project Editors: Eve Marleau and
Starry Dog
Designers: Starry Dog and
Nikki Kenwood
Illustrator: Mike Byrne

Published in the United States by
QEB Publishing, Inc.
3 Wrigley, Suite A
Irvine, CA 92618

www.qeb-publishing.com

ISBN 978 1 59566 805 9

A CIP record for this book is available
from the Library of Congress.

Printed in China

Picture credits
Key: t = top, b = bottom, l = left,
r = right, c = centre, FC = front cover,
BC = back cover.

1: Mark Higgins/iStockphoto; 2-3:
Markross/Dreamstime; 4: t Tim Laman/
Getty, b David Knowles/ Fotolibra; 5:
Roine Magnusson/Getty; 6-7: all images
Shutterstock; 8: t Dr Rafe M. Brown, b
Wells Bert & Babs; 9: Gary Bell/zefa/
Corbis; 10: Shutterstock; 12: t Rod
Planck/ iStockphoto, b Nigel J. Dennis/
Gallo Images/Corbis; 13: Gavriel Jecan/
Corbis; 14: Shutterstock; 15: Rod Planck/
iStockphoto, Nigel J. Dennis/Gallo
Images/ Corbis, br Shutterstock; 16: t
Hans Reinhard/zefa/ Corbis, b Nicholas
Smythe/ iStockphoto; 17: David M. Dennis/
Photolibrary; 18: tr Hans Reinhard/zefa/
Corbis, bl Nicholas Smythe/iStockphoto,
all other images Shutterstock; 19: t
Nicholas Smythe/ iStockphoto, c Hans
Reinhard/zefa/ Corbis, b Shutterstock;
20: t Wolfgang_Thieme /dpa/Corbis, b
James Richey/iStockphoto; 21: Elzbieta
Sekowska/iStockphoto; 22: l Shutterstock,
c James Richey/iStockphoto, r Wolfgang_
Thieme/dpa/Corbis; 24: t Marshall Bruce/
iStockphoto, b Winfried Wisniewski/
zefa/ Corbis; 25: Peter Johnson/ Corbis;
27: Shutterstock; 28: t Craig Aurness/
Corbis, b Shutterstock; 29: Philip
Date/ Shutterstock; 30-31: all images
Shutterstock; 32: t Gary Bell/zefa/Corbis, b
Lori Froeb/Shutterstock; 33: Mark Higgins/
iStockphoto; 35: all images Shutterstock;
36: t W. Perry Conway/Corbis, b Professor
Phil Myers/Corbis; 37: Gary Braasch/
Corbis; 38-39: all images Shutterstock; 40:
t Bruce Robison/Corbis, b Bruce Robison/
Corbis; 41: Visual&Written SL/Alamy; 42:
Shutterstock; 44: t Max Gibbs/Photolibrary,
b Norbert Wu/Getty; 45: Norbert Wu/
Getty; 46: Norbert Wu/Getty; 48: t Juergen
Schraml/Hippocampus Bildrachiv, b Hal
Beral/Corbis; 49: Dzain/Dreamstime;
50: Shutterstock; 52: t Gary Bell/Getty,
b Fredrik Ehrenstrom/Photolibrary; 53:
Dan Schmitt/iStockphoto; 55: all images
Shutterstock; 56: t Steve McWilliam/
Shutterstock, b Shutterstock; 57: Nigel
Cattlin/ Holt Studios International/Science
Photo Library; 58: all images Shutterstock;
60: t Pufferfishy/ Dreamstime, b Stuart
Westmorland/Getty; 61 Roger Horrocks/
Getty; 62: l Pufferfishy/Dreamstime, c
Shutterstock, r Stuart Westmorland/Getty;
64: bl George Africa, bl Tony Baggett/
Dreamstime, 64–65: t Michael & Patricia
Fogden/Corbis, b Michael & Patricia
Fogden/Corbis; 68: t Philippe Psaila/Science
Photo Library, b Joe McDonald/Corbis;
69: Michael & Patricia Fogden/Corbis;
71: all images Shutterstock; 72: t Thomas
Mounsey/Shutterstock, b Holt Studios
International Ltd/Alamy; 73: blickwinkel/
Alamy; 74-75: all images Shutterstock; 76:
t Klaus Nilkens/iStockphoto, b Dr Morley
Read/Shutterstock; 77: Snowleopardl/
Shutterstock; 80: Joe McDonald/Corbis;
81: t Bob Kupbens/iStockphoto, b Mark
Moffett/Getty; 84: t Claus Meyer/Getty,
b Wikipedia; 85: Pete Oxford/Getty; 88: t
Olga Bogatyrenko/Shutterstock, b Arthur
Morris/Corbis; 89: Juniors Bildarchiv/
Alamy; 92-93: b Frans Lanting/Corbis; 93:
t Timothy Martin/iStockphoto, b Daniel
Heuclin/NHPA/Photoshot; 94-95: all
images Shutterstock; 96: t Patti Murray/
Photolibrary, b John Pitcher/iStockphoto;
97 Katherine Haluska/Big Stock Photo;
98: Shutterstock; 99: Shutterstock; 100: t
Stuart Elflett/Big Stock Photo, b Pixelman/
Dreamstime; 101: Fishguy66/Dreamstime;
102-103: all images Shutterstock; 104:
bl Florian Schulz/Alamy, 104-105:
Michal Boubin/Big Stock Photo; 105:
br WildPictures/Alamy; 108: Fouroaks/
Dreamstime; 109: t Leslie Garland Picture
Library/Alamy, b Jorge Pedro Barradas
de Casais/Shutterstock; 110: Shutterstock;
111: Shutterstock; 112: t Pufferfishy/
Dreamstime, b Xenobug/Dreamstime; 113
DK Limited/Corbis; 114: Shutterstock; 115:
Shutterstock.

The words in **bold** are
explained in the glossary on
page 116.

WARNING
Where you see this
symbol, ask
an adult
for help.

Contents

Smelly animals

Some animals really stink, but often there is a reason for it. A smell can help an animal to find a mate, or it may help to keep predators away.

Moonrats use their long noses to smell if other moonrats have been in their territory.

Moonrats

Moonrats live in the rainforests and swamps of South East Asia. They mark their **den** with a liquid that smells like rotting onions. This warns other moonrats and predators to stay away.

Polecats

Polecats live in parts of Europe, Asia, and North Africa. They mark their territory with a nasty-smelling liquid, which is made in the **glands** at the bottom of their tails.

Polecats hunt at night. Their sense of smell helps them sniff out prey in the dark.

Foul fact!

About 100 years ago, musk oxen were almost extinct because of hunting. It is now against the law to hunt them.

Musk ox

The musk ox lives in cold parts of the world, such as Greenland and Canada. Males, or bulls, make a smelly liquid in glands just under their eyes. This liquid attracts females, who can smell it from far away.

▶ The musk ox has long hair to keep it warm in cold weather.

COUNT IT!

Smell the odd one out!

There are two of each animal. Circle the stinky odd one out, then write how many pairs of animals you can see in the box.

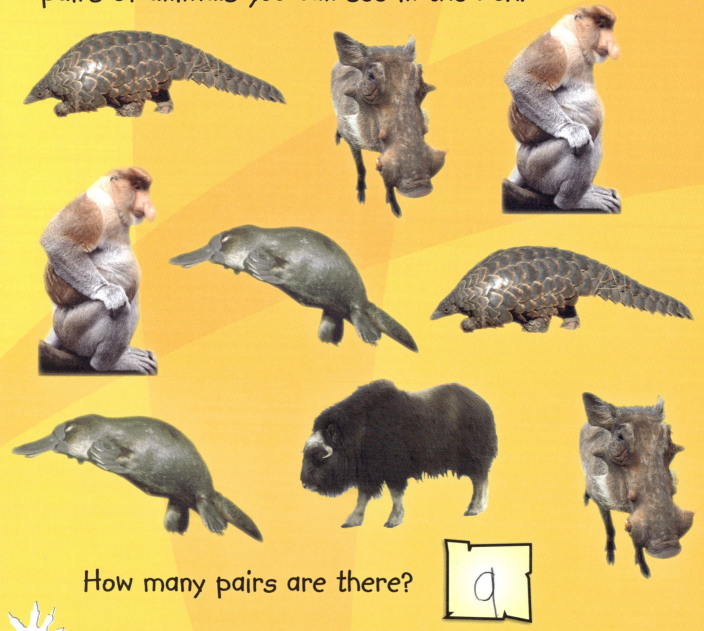

How many pairs are there?

9

Smelly sums

Add up the stinky animals. Write your answers in the boxes.

Animal Stickers

Some animals have sticky parts. Sticky tongues help some animals catch food. Other animals stick to things using **suction**.

▲ To scare predators, the black-spotted sticky frog puffs itself up and shows its back, which has two large spots on it. This makes the frog look like a snake's head.

Black-spotted sticky frog

The black-spotted sticky frog lives in the rainforests of South East Asia. The frog makes a sticky slime when it is scared to stop predators from eating it.

Numbat

The numbat, or banded anteater, uses its nose to find **termite mounds**. When it finds one, the numbat pokes its long, sticky tongue into the mound to catch the termites.

◀ The numbat eats about 20,000 termites every day.

Crown-of-thorns starfish

The crown-of-thorns starfish lives in
warm seas. The starfish has thousands
of tiny feet to help it move around.
The feet have suction cups that help
it to cling to rocks.

▼ The crown-of-thorns starfish is
covered in poisonous spines.

Get arty with grids

Using the grid, copy the picture of a sticky frog into the larger grid below. Color in your sticky frog.

Starfish hunt

Can you circle five differences between these starfish?

Do you know how many legs the Antarctic starfish has?

Find the answer on page 120

Nasty noses

The star-nosed mole is blind, so its tentacles help it feel for food.

Some animals have amazing noses, which they use to find food. They may smell their **prey** from far away, or use their noses to feel for movements made by prey.

Star-nosed mole

The star-nosed mole of North America has 22 fleshy tentacles that stick out from its nose. They help the mole to feel movement in the ground made by its prey, such as worms.

Aardvark

The aardvark lives in southern Africa. It has a long **snout**, which it uses to sniff out ants and termites to eat as it walks along. It may walk as far as 18 miles (30 kilometers) in one night.

When an aardvark breaks into a termite mound, it can squeeze its nose shut to keep out dust.

▶ Proboscis monkeys walk on their back legs, unlike most monkeys, who walk using all four legs.

Foul fact!

A male proboscis monkey pushes its nose out of the way when it eats!

Proboscis monkey

The proboscis monkey is named after the large, wobbly nose, or "proboscis," of the male monkey. It is thought that the large nose helps the male attract a female. The nose of the male can be up to 6 inches (14 centimeters) long.

WORD SCRAMBLE

Stinky word search

Find the words in the word search below that have to do with smelly animals. Use the word bank to help you.

MOONRAT   DEN   BULL   OX
SWAMPS   SMELL   HAIR   STINKY

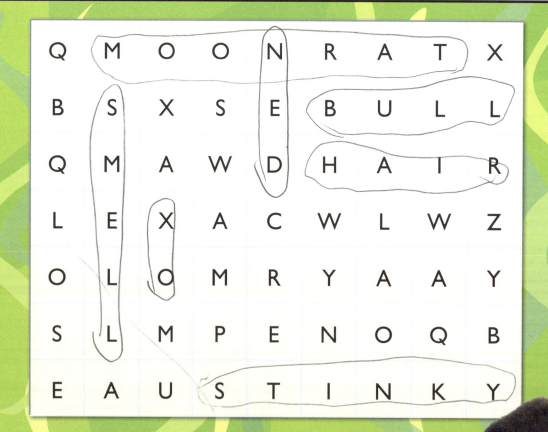

Q M O O N R A T X
B S X S E B U L L
Q M A W D H A I R
L E X A C W L W Z
O L O M R Y A A Y
S L M P E N O Q B
E A U S T I N K Y

14

Mix and match

Draw a line to connect the unusual feature to each animal. Some animals have more than one feature.

proboscis monkey

snout

tentacles

nose

aardvark

walks on two legs

star mole

eats termites and ants

Poisonous animals

There are many poisonous animals around the world. Some animals use **venom**, or poison, to protect themselves. Others use it to catch prey.

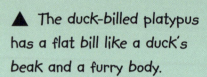

▲ The duck-billed platypus has a flat bill like a duck's beak and a furry body.

Duck-billed platypus

The duck-billed platypus lives in eastern Australia. The male platypus has a **spur**, or point, on each of its back legs, which holds poison. If the platypus is scared, it stabs its enemy with the spur and injects the poison. The poison is so strong it could kill an animal as big as a dog.

Solenodons

The two species of solenodon are both **endangered**. They live on islands in the Caribbean Sea. A solenodon has poisonous **saliva**, or spit. When it attacks prey, such as spiders, the solenodon's poisonous saliva stops it from moving, making it easier to hold on to.

◀ Solenodons run on their toes. They often fall over if they run too fast.

Pit vipers

The diamondback rattlesnake is a type of pit viper, or venomous snake. They know when prey is nearby because they can sense, or feel, heat from the prey's body. This helps them catch food at night. When they bite down, they inject poison into their prey through their fangs.

▼ The venom of a diamondback rattlesnake is used to make a medicine for snake bites.

Foul fact!

Many pit vipers are hunted and killed for their skin, which is used to make shoes and belts.

Number crunching

Write the word that shows the correct number of the poisonous animals in the boxes below each picture. Use the number bank to help you.

one   two   three   four   five   six   eight

two

five

one

four

Do you know why platypus are different from other mammals?

six

eight

three

Find the answer on page 120

Ugly brutes

Some animals look ugly. They may have no hair, or have lumps on their faces, or big noses. Although they look strange, these parts can help the animals survive.

▲ Naked mole rats' small eyes and ears are almost hidden in the folds of their skin.

Naked mole rat

The naked mole rat lives in underground tunnels in eastern Africa. It lives in groups of 20 to 300 mole rats. The naked mole rat has no hair to stop it from getting too hot when it is underground.

▼ Male elephant seals have big noses that they use to make roaring noises. This helps them attract females.

Elephant seals

Elephant seals have many folds of fat and skin. Their thick layer of fat is called blubber. This keeps them warm when they dive into the ocean to search for food.

A warthog uses its canine teeth to dig and search for food.

▼ The four bumps help protect the warthog's face when it fights.

Warthog

The warthog lives in Africa. The male warthog has four hard bumps on its face that look like warts. The warthog also has tusks that grow out of its mouth. It uses them as weapons when it fights other warthogs.

Who am I?

Can you answer these questions? Write the answers on the writing lines. Look at page 20 for some clues.

I have bumps on my face that help me find food. _____

I have folds of fat and skin that make me look rumpled. _____

I have small eyes and ears that are hidden in the folds of my skin. _____

warthog

elephant seal

naked mole rat

Ugly scramble!

Unscramble the words that have to do with ugly animals. Use the word bank to help you. Write your answers on the lines.

ugly   naked   wart   skin   nose

osen   _____

dnake   _____

wtra   _____

insk   _____

lyug   _____

Foul feeders

Birds such as vultures eat **carrion**, or dead animals. The body of a dead animal is called a carcass. Some birds regurgitate, or bring up, food to put off **predators**. Others do it to feed their babies.

▲ The hoatzin cannot fly well. It spends a lot of time perching as it digests its meal.

Hoatzin

The hoatzin, or "stinky cowbird," smells like cow poop. The smell comes from the **bacteria** in its stomach that helps the bird to digest food. The smell is so strong that predators do not want to eat it.

Gannets

Gannets are seabirds. They eat fish and squid. Gannets regurgitate their food if they are scared by something or if they are feeding their young.

◀ A baby gannet will tap its mother's beak to get her to regurgitate food.

Vultures

Vultures are **scavengers**—they eat dead animals that have been killed by predators, such as lions. Vultures have strong acid in their stomachs to help them digest food. Some vultures can even digest bones.

Foul fact!

Most vultures do not have feathers on their heads. It would be difficult to keep them clean when they eat.

◀ Different types of vulture sometimes feed on the same carcass. White-headed vultures rip open the carcass, white-backed vultures eat the insides, and lappet-faced vultures finish the leftovers.

Who's who?

Draw a line to match the shapes to the correct foul feeder. Color them in, using pages 24 and 25 to help you.

gannet

hoatzin

vulture

Fly home!

Help the vulture make its way through the maze to find its nest.

Freaky flyers

Birds come in all shapes and sizes, from tiny hummingbirds to huge birds of prey. Birds are not the only animals that fly. Bats and insects fly, too.

▼ Hummingbirds hover in the air to feed from flowers. Some **species** do this by flapping their wings about 50 times per second.

▲ Many birds carry food to their young in their stomach and then regurgitate, or bring up, the food for its babies to eat.

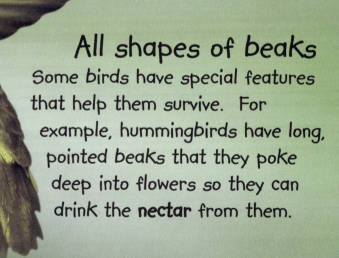

All shapes of beaks

Some birds have special features that help them survive. For example, hummingbirds have long, pointed beaks that they poke deep into flowers so they can drink the **nectar** from them.

Horrible habits

Some birds have horrible habits, such as regurgitating food for their babies to eat. Some bats have horrible habits, too. The vampire bat drinks the blood of other animals. Other bats, such as fruit bats, or flying foxes, only eat fruit.

▲ After eating fruit, the fruit bat licks its claws clean.

COUNT IT!

Hummingbird hover

How many hummingbirds are feeding at each flower? Write the answers in the boxes below.

1

2

2

4

4

Hummingbird sums

Do these hummingbird sums, then
write the answers in the boxes.

Big mouth

Some birds, such as pelicans, have a huge mouth that they use to catch prey. Other birds use their mouths to scare predators.

▲ A tawny frogmouth opens its beak and shows its yellow throat to scare predators.

Tawny frogmouth

The tawny frogmouth lives in Australia. During the day, it sits still in trees. At night, it hunts for insects. The tawny frogmouth either kills its prey first or swallows it whole.

Toucans

Toucans live in the rain forests of South America. They use their huge, colorful bills to pick fruit to eat. Their long bills can reach fruit on branches from far away. Toucans try to attract mates by throwing fruit at each other.

◄ The toucan's large bill can also scare off predators from eating them.

Pelicans

Pelicans are water birds found by the sea. A large pouch hangs under their beak. They eat animals such as fish, frogs, and crabs. Sometimes they also eat smaller birds.

▼ Pelicans use their throat pouch to scoop prey out of the water.

Foul fact!
In the past, people thought mother pelicans fed their young with their own blood when there was no food.

ALL ABOUT BIRDS

Toucan color, too!

Finish coloring in the toucan. Use the smaller image to help you.

WOW! Toucans are very noisy. Their call sounds like the croaking of frogs!

Pelican jumble

Circle the pelican that is the odd one out.

Beastly bats

Many bats look very strange. Although some people are scared of bats, they Aactually do a lot of good by eating harmful insects.

The fringe-lipped bat gets its name from the lumps on its face.

Fringe-lipped bat

The fringe-lipped bat mainly eats frogs. Fringe-lipped bats can tell which frogs are poisonous and which are not by the sounds the frogs make when they are looking for a mate.

Wrinkle-faced bat

The wrinkle-faced bat has lots of folds of skin on its face. The bat lives in trees by day. At night, it eats fruit such as bananas.

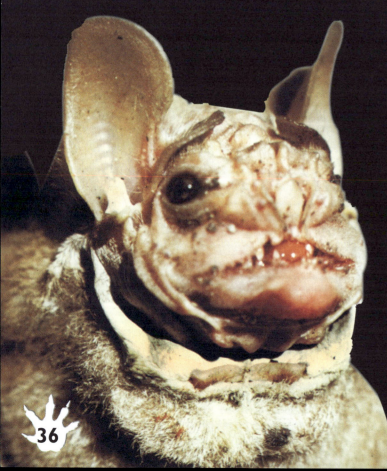

◀ When the bat wants to rest, it pulls up some skin from its chin and hooks it over the top of its head.

Spectral bat

The spectral bat is one of the largest bats in the world. It has a wingspan of up to 3 feet (one meter). The spectral bat hunts at night for birds, small mammals, reptiles, frogs, large insects, and fruit—and even other bats! Spectral bats drop down from trees onto their prey as it moves below them.

Foul fact!

Father spectral bats often sleep with the mother and baby bat wrapped in their wings.

▲ The spectral bat has long front teeth that it uses to eat its prey.

SPELL IT!

All about bats

Trace these words about bats.
Write them on the lines below.

bat

bat have wings.

prey

wings

hunt

night

38

Bat talk

Finish these sentences about bats.
Use the word bank to help you.

wings	night	hunt	bat	prey

Bats hunt at _____ night _____.

Bats have wide _____ wings _____.

Bats _____ hunt _____ insects.

Bats hunt other _____ prey _____
such as frogs and birds.

A spectral _____ bat _____
is one of the largest bats in
the world.

Terrors of the deep

There are some very strange fish at the bottom of the ocean. Some have terrifying teeth. Others even have eyes that point upward!

▲ Marine hatchetfish live in the Atlantic, Pacific, and Indian oceans.

Spookfish

Some types of spookfish are also called barreleyes because its eyes are tube-shaped. Barreleyes live between 1,300 and 8,200 feet (400 and 2,500 meters) below the surface of the ocean. Their eyes point upward and help them see **predators** in the dark water.

Marine hatchetfish

Marine hatchetfish live between 650 and 19,700 feet (200 and 6000 meters) below the surface of the ocean. They have small cells on the undersides of their bodies that look like tiny lights. These lights may help them to attract and catch prey.

◀ A barreleye's skull is so thin that you can see its brain.

▶ The barbeled dragonfish is about 6 inches (15 centimeters) long.

Barbeled dragonfish

Barbeled dragonfish live in depths of up to 4,900 feet (1,500 meters). The female has a long barbel, or stalk. The barbel has a light on the tip, and the fish can flash the light on and off. When prey comes closer to see what the light is, the fish gobbles it up.

Foul fact!

The young of some dragonfish have eyes on the end of long stalks.

Tooth terror

The barbeled dragonfish is a fierce fish with scary teeth. Make this barbeled dragon extra fierce by drawing its scary teeth.

Is anyone down there?

Here is a scene showing some of the fish that live at the bottom of the ocean. Draw your own fish in this sea scene. Color the fish in.

Vicious vampires

▼ The candirú's body is almost see-through. This makes it hard to spot in the water.

Vampires are not only around at Halloween! Some types of fish also suck blood from other creatures.

Candirú

The candirú is a tiny fish that lives in the Amazon River. To find its prey, it tastes the water to see if it is coming through the **gills** of another fish. It finds the fish and slips inside its gills. Spines around the candirú's head dig into the fish and hold the candirú in place so it can feed on the fish's blood.

▼ Viperfish hunt at night in shallow water. They return to much deeper water by day.

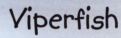

Viperfish

A viperfish's sharp, fanglike teeth are so long that they do not fit inside its mouth. The viperfish swims quickly toward its prey and uses its teeth to stab its victims.

Common fangtooth

The common fangtooth is a really scary-looking deep-sea fish. It gets its name from the sharp fangs that stick out of its enormous mouth. It might look scary, but it mainly eats tiny **zooplankton**.

▶ When the common fangtooth shuts its mouth, the two long teeth on the bottom jaw slip into two tubes in its top jaw.

Foul fact!

The common fangtooth is so ugly that its nickname is "ogrefish"!

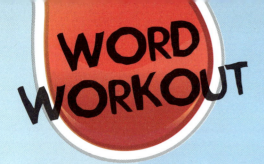

WORD WORKOUT

Missing letters

Fill in the first and last letter of each word about vicious vampires. Use the letter bank to help you.

F H H M H V T S H E H D

F A N G T O O T H

M O U T H

V I P E R F I S H

_ E E T _

_ P I K _

H E A D

Vampire word search

Now find the words in the word search.
Use the word bank to help you.

VIPERFISH   FANGTOOTH   SPIKE

HEAD   MOUTH

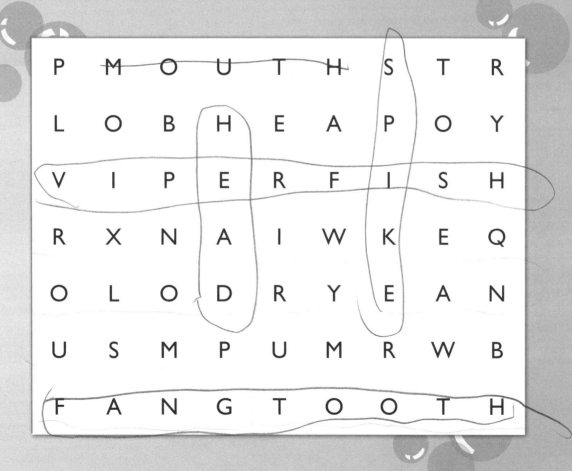

P M O U T H S T R

L O B H E A P O Y

V I P E R F I S H

R X N A I W K E Q

O L O D R Y E A N

U S M P U M R W B

F A N G T O O T H

Hard to spot

Fish have some very clever disguises. Some look like lumps of stone, others look like pieces of seaweed.

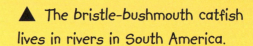

▲ The bristle-bushmouth catfish lives in rivers in South America.

▼ The devil scorpionfish looks as if it has weeds growing on it. Its skin changes color to match where it is living.

Bristle-bushmouth catfish

The bristle-bushmouth catfish lives in rivers. It has long tentacles on its snout, which it uses to find food. It is sometimes called the Medusa Head. In Greek mythology, Medusa was a woman who had snakes for hair.

Devil scorpionfish

The devil scorpionfish disguises itself to look like a rock or coral. The fish has **venomous** spines on its back and fins that it uses to defend itself. The poison can kill humans.

Leafy sea dragon

The leafy sea dragon lives in the oceans around Australia. The leafy shapes on the sea dragon help it hide in floating seaweed or kelp beds.

▶ The leafy sea dragon is related to sea horses.

HIDE AND SEEK

Spot the yarn

Find out how camouflage works with this fun experiment.

You will need:
- Watch with second hand or stopwatch
- 5 pieces of yarn, around 2 inches (5 centimeters) long in green, yellow, blue, red, and black (25 pieces in total)

1. Choose a patch of grass in a park or yard for an adult to place the yarn in.

2. Ask an adult to put the pieces of yarn in a patch of grass. Don't watch them!

3. See how many pieces of yarn you can find in one minute.

4. Which colors were easiest to find? Which were hardest? Write down the order in which you found the yarn in the table below.

Pieces of yarn

green	
yellow	
blue	
red	
black	

What happened?

The green and yellow pieces of yarn were the hardest to find because they blended in with the color of the grass, just as an animal blends into its background through camouflage. The red, blue, and black were probably the easiest to find because they look very different from grass.

Poisonous parts

Many fish and other water animals are poisonous. Most of them only use their poison to protect themselves from other creatures.

Weevers

Weevers have poisonous spines on their gills and on a fin on their back. During the day, weevers bury themselves in the sand on the seabed. As shrimp and small fish swim past, the weevers snap them up.

▲ The blue-ringed octopus is one of the world's most poisonous animals.

Blue-ringed octopuses

Blue-ringed octopuses live in tide pools in the Pacific Ocean. If a predator comes close, it turns bright yellow with blue rings, bites the attacker, and injects it with poison. One octopus carries enough poison to kill 26 adults.

◄ If a person stood on a weever, the fish's spines would sink into their foot. This would release a poison.

▼ It can be very difficult to spot among the reef's rocks.

Stonefish

The stonefish lives on coral reefs in the shallow tropical waters of the Indian and Pacific oceans. The stonefish is the most venomous fish in the world. The fin on its back is covered in many venomous spines.

Foul fact!

Poison from the stonefish causes very severe pain and can kill humans.

Color by numbers

The blue-ringed octopus turns blue and yellow when it is attacked by a predator. Color blue the spaces marked with 1. Color yellow the spaces marked with 2.

1. blue
2. yellow

Stonefish spotting

Spot the stonefish in these pictures.
Write down how many stonefish
you can see in the box.

Sticky slugs

Slug slime helps to stop slugs' skin from drying out. It also makes traveling across the ground easier. The slime can even make predators' tongues go numb, which may stop them from eating slugs.

▲ The black slug covers itself in a thick foul-tasting slime, which protects it against predators.

Black slug

The black slug can be different colors, too, such as brown and white. It is often active during the day, when other slugs are hiding from the sun under rocks and leaves. Black slugs mainly eat dead plants.

▼ Leopard slugs can grow up to 8 inches (20 centimeters) long.

Leopard slug

The leopard slug is common in the UK and Ireland. It also lives along the coasts of North America. The leopard slug disguises itself with spots and stripes to hide from predators.

Gray field slug

The gray field slug spends its life above ground feeding on plants, unlike most slugs, which spend a lot of their time in the earth. Like other slugs, it eats twice its body weight in food every day.

▶ The gray field slug's slime is usually clear, but when the slug is scared the slime becomes thick, white, and sticky.

How does your garden grow?

You can find slugs in gardens or other places where lots of plants grow. In the garden below, circle the leopard slugs, gray field slugs, and black slugs with different colored crayons.

Slug graph

Color the number of squares that show how many leopard slugs, gray field slugs, and black slugs are in the garden.

number of slugs

leopard slugs · field slugs · black slugs

Squishy sea life

Some sea creatures have very soft bodies. Animals that are too squishy to live on land can survive in the ocean because they are supported by the water.

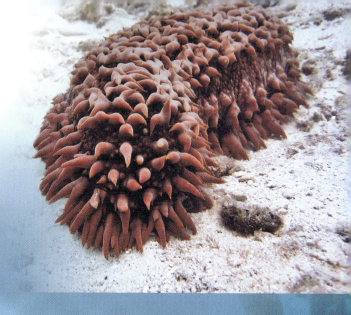

▲ A sea cucumber has hundreds of sticky feet that it uses to crawl around on the seabed.

Sea cucumbers

Sea cucumbers have warty skin and soft spines. When they are frightened, some sea cucumbers even shoot out their **intestines** at predators to scare them off. They then grow new intestines.

Sea anemones

Sea anemones can be as small as 0.5 inches (1.25 centimeters), and some as big as 6 feet (1.8 meters). Their mouth is in the center, surrounded by tentacles. These tentacles are used to catch and kill prey. When they touch the prey, the tentacles fire a tiny spike into it and inject it with poison.

◄ The sea anemone's tentacles help it to catch prey, such as small fish.

Box jellyfish

Box jellyfish are sometimes called sea wasps. One very poisonous species is about the size of a basketball. It has long tentacles that drift behind it as it swims. The tentacles' sting can kill prey, such as shrimp and fish.

▼ It is thought that box jellyfish may have killed more than 5,500 people since 1954.

Foul fact!

The venom from some box jellyfish can kill a human in less than 4 minutes!

WORD WIZARD

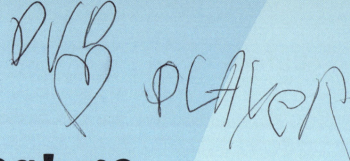

Creature feature

Match the feature to the correct creature.

long tentacles

warts

short tentacles

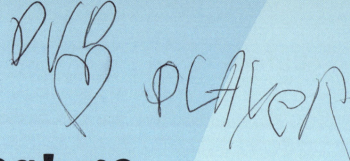

62

Squishy word search

Find the words in the word search that have to do with squishy sea life. Use the word bank to help you.

FIN   SPINES

TENTACLES   SPIKE

B	Z	H	J	Q	S	E	V	C
T	E	N	T	A	C	L	E	S
E	C	H	I	D	N	A	E	H
J	U	D	B	T	B	S	K	Q
M	Q	B	F	N	E	E	N	R
O	K	A	I	I	A	N	O	W
L	E	T	N	G	R	I	M	I
S	P	I	K	E	K	P	A	X
M	L	S	U	V	D	S	D	Y

Soil sliders

Foul fact!

A flatworm gets rid of its poo through the same hole that it uses to take in food.

Some slimy creatures use their slimy **feces**, or poop, as a disguise. Others make a poisonous slime to keep predators away, and some simply use their slime to help them move.

▼ Lily beetle larvae eat lily leaves, starting at the tips and working their way back to the stem of the leaf.

Lily beetle larva

The larva of the scarlet lily beetle is very slimy. It hatches from its egg and covers itself in its own wet, slimy feces, so that it looks a bit like bird poo. This helps to keep it safe from predators.

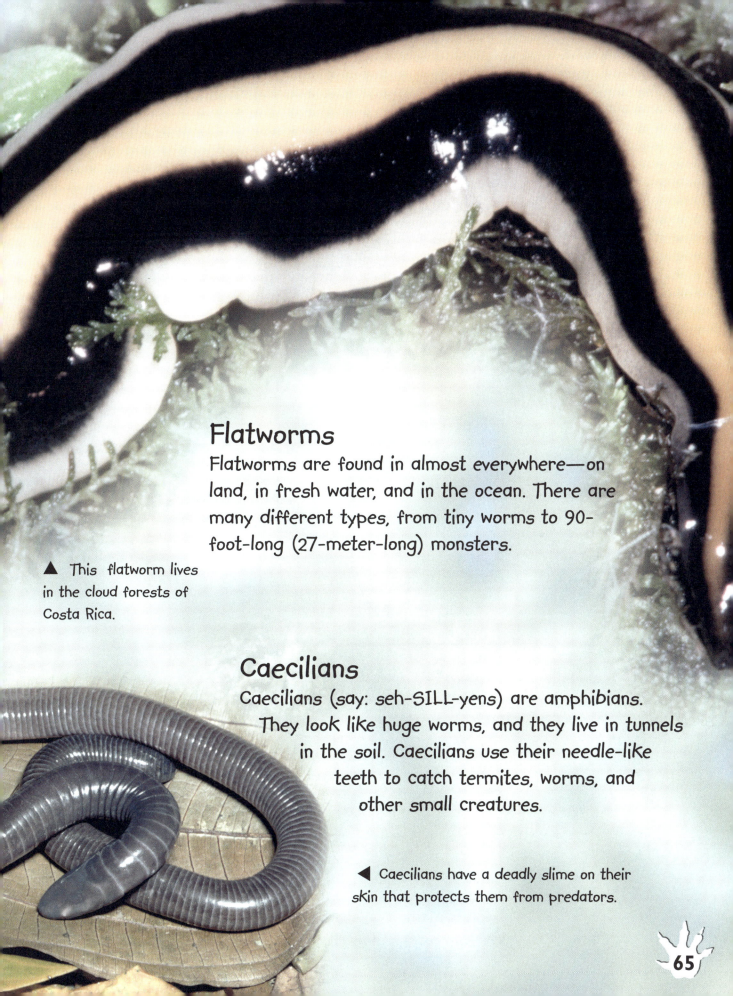

Flatworms

Flatworms are found in almost everywhere—on land, in fresh water, and in the ocean. There are many different types, from tiny worms to 90-foot-long (27-meter-long) monsters.

▲ This flatworm lives in the cloud forests of Costa Rica.

Caecilians

Caecilians (say: seh-SILL-yens) are amphibians. They look like huge worms, and they live in tunnels in the soil. Caecilians use their needle-like teeth to catch termites, worms, and other small creatures.

◄ Caecilians have a deadly slime on their skin that protects them from predators.

MOVE IT!

WARNING

Soil sliders

Find out how earthworms move with this fun experiment.

You will need:

- A loose spring, such as a slinky toy
- A smooth surface, such as a desktop

1. Put the spring on a table.

2. Hold the ends with your hands.

? Do you know how many hearts an earthworm has?

Find the answer on page 120

3. Use your right hand to pull one end of the spring.

4. Release the spring from your left hand.

5. The spring should move forward a few inches from where it was.

What happened?

An earthworm works in the same ways as the spring—it stretches out first and then moves by pulling its muscles more tightly together.

Slimy amphibians

Amphibians spend some of the time on land and some of the time in water. They have to keep their skin damp and slimy.

Slimy salamanders

Slimy salamanders do not have lungs like humans. They breathe in air through their skin. Slimy salamanders get their name from the slime on their skin. If you get it on your hands, it sticks like glue.

▼ The sticky slime that slimy salamanders make stops predators from eating them.

▲ The olm is also called the humanfish because its skin looks like human skin.

Olm

The olm lives in caves in parts of Europe. It is albino, which means it has no color at all in its skin. It is also blind, but has good hearing and sense of smell. The olm eats crabs, snails, and bugs.

Gray foam-nest treefrog

The gray foam-nest treefrog lives in Africa. Foam-nest treefrogs save water in their bodies so that they can live in very dry places. They also create a slime that makes their skin waterproof.

Gray foam-nest treefrogs make their foam nest on a branch over pools. Tadpoles hatch, and a week later drop into the water below.

Foul fact!
The gray foam-nest treefrog turns almost white in hot weather. This helps keep the frog cool.

Salamander match up

Circle the salamander that is different from the others. Color it in.

Find the treefrogs!

There are 10 treefrogs hiding in the forest below.
Find them and circle them.

Slimy bugs

Some slimy creatures can mean trouble for humans. Millipedes and froghoppers can damage plants. Maggots are useful to fishermen, but their parent flies can carry diseases.

Maggots

"Maggot" is the name given to fly larvae. Some types of maggot, such as botfly larvae, are parasites. They live under the skin of living animals, causing sores, cuts, and even death.

▼ The spotted snake millipede needs to stay damp and slimy.

Foul fact!

Millipedes prefer to live in ground that has been covered in manure, or animal poop.

Snake millipedes

Snake millipedes live in dead leaves, under bark, and in moss. Snake millipedes use their 200 legs to climb trees to find food. They sometimes find their way into houses, too.

Froghoppers

Froghoppers are small brown insects that can jump 28 inches (70 centimeters) through the air to reach the next plant. Their larvae are called **nymphs**. For protection, the nymphs develop inside a *blob* of froth, called cuckoo spit. The froth hides the nymph from predators and *stops* it from getting too hot or cold.

◀ A froghopper nymph is also known as a spittlebug.

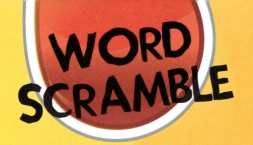

WORD SCRAMBLE

Slimy scramble

Match the *scrambled* word that has to do with slimy *bugs* in the first column to the correct word in the second column.

gotmag	millipede
pedemilli	froghopper
ppoerhrfog	maggot
mphny	froth
othfr	nymph
imysl	spittlebug
butlegspit	damp
lesg	slimy
mpda	legs

Word up

Now find the words on page 74 in the word search below.

E	Z	H	S	Q	S	E	L	E	G	S
D	E	N	P	A	G	L	X	S	R	W
E	C	H	I	D	N	A	E	H	A	F
P	U	D	T	T	F	R	O	T	H	Z
I	Q	B	T	N	E	T	N	R	I	E
L	K	S	L	I	M	Y	Y	W	K	C
L	E	T	E	G	R	I	M	I	B	M
I	P	I	B	E	K	D	P	X	T	A
M	L	S	U	V	D	A	H	Y	U	I
M	A	G	G	O	T	M	Z	M	L	Q
F	R	O	G	H	O	P	P	E	R	K

Cold blood!

Animals such as lizards, snakes, and crocodiles are all types of reptile. Creatures such as frogs and salamanders are called amphibians. **Amphibians** and reptiles are cold-blooded animals, which means that their bodies are the same temperature as the air around them.

▲ Like crocodiles, the dinosaur T-rex had sharp teeth for grabbing food.

Reptiles old and new

Dinosaurs were reptiles that lived millions of years ago. Like modern reptiles, they had no fur and they hatched from eggs. Dinosaurs are now **extinct.**

◀ The Ecuador mushroomtongue salamander does not breathe through lungs like humans. It breathes through its skin.

Amphibians

Amphibians have **adapted,** or changed, to live both in and out of water. They can breathe through their skin, but most adult amphibians also have lungs for breathing. Many amphibians pretend to be dead if there is a predator around so that they will be left alone. Some amphibians make **toxins** in their skin so they taste bad to predators.

◀ Poison-dart frogs have poisonous skin. Tribespeople in South America rub the frogs against parrots. The poison makes the parrots grow different-colored feathers.

COLOR IT!

Color crazy!

Poison-dart frogs are brightly colored.
Color the poison-dart frog below.

Then color the parrot in the colors that it might turn if a poison-dart frog was rubbed against it.

Poisonous pests

Some reptiles and amphibians are poisonous. They might have poison in their skin, their saliva, or their fangs.

▼ The horned viper has two long scales on its head that look like horns. The horns help protect the snake's eyes.

Horned viper

When hunting, the horned viper digs its body into the sand and lies in wait. The only parts of the snake that can be seen are its horns. When prey is near, it comes out of the sand and shoots a poison from its fangs into the animal. The horned viper eats rats, as well as small snakes, lizards, and birds.

A drug made from the saliva of the Gila monster is being used in the United States to treat diabetes.

▲ The Gila monster has powerful claws for digging burrows, or tunnels.

Gila monster

The Gila monster is a lizard. It kills and eats birds, rodents, and other lizards by biting them and chewing until venomous saliva flows into the animal. If the Gila monster's teeth get broken, it just grows some more.

Poison-dart frogs

Poison-dart frogs are found in Central and South America. Most are brightly colored to warn predators no to eat them. Poison is released, or comes out of, their skin.

81

Spots and stripes!

Poison-dart frogs are brightly colored with spots and stripes. How many spots and stripes does each frog have?

_____ stripes, _____ spots.

_____ stripes, _____ spots.

_____ stripes, _____ spots.

_____ stripes, _____ spots.

Do you know where poison-dart frogs live in the rain forest?

_____ stripes, _____ spots.

_____ stripes, _____ spots.

_____ stripes, _____ spots.

_____ stripes, _____ spots.

Find the answer on page 120

Funky frogs

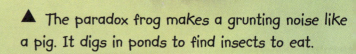

Frogs live all over the world. Most **species**, or types, live in **tropical** countries with warm, wetter climates, but some prefer hot deserts.

▼ The pouched frog is about the size of a cherry.

▲ The paradox frog makes a grunting noise like a pig. It digs in ponds to find insects to eat.

Paradox frog

The paradox frog lives in ponds and lakes in South America and Trinidad. Adult paradox frogs are about 2 inches (6 centimeters) long, but their **tadpoles** are much larger, at up to 9 inches (22 centimeters) long. As the tadpoles develop into adults, they get smaller.

Pouched frog

The pouched frog lives in Australia. The female lays a pile of eggs in soil rather than in water. As the eggs hatch into tadpoles, the male hops into the middle of the pile, and the tadpoles wriggle into two pouches just above his back legs. The tadpoles stay in his pouches until they grow into small frogs.

Foul fact!

In Bolivia and Peru, some people like to eat Lake Titicaca frogs.

Lake Titicaca frog

The Lake Titicaca frog lives only in Lake Titicaca in South America. Lake Titicaca is 12,500 feet (3,812 meters) above the ocean. At this height, the air has less oxygen, which all animals need to breathe. The Lake Titicaca frog has saggy skin with many folds. As the frog breathes through its skin, these extra folds help it to breathe in more oxygen.

▼ The Lake Titicaca frog can also breathe underwater. It sometimes does strange "press-ups" that disturb the water and make more oxygen flow.

Write on!

Trace these words that have to do with frogs. Try writing them yourself on the lines below.

tadpole

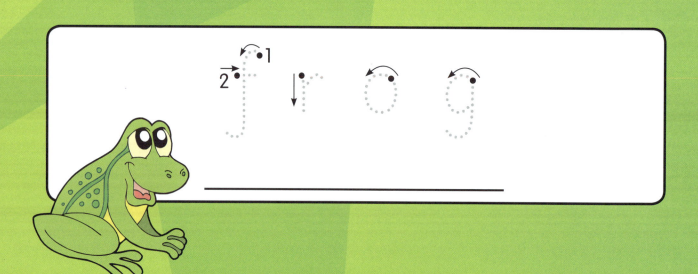

frog

Frog word search

Using the word bank to help you, find the words in the search below.

SPECIES	FROG	LAKE
BREATHE	SKIN	TADPOLE

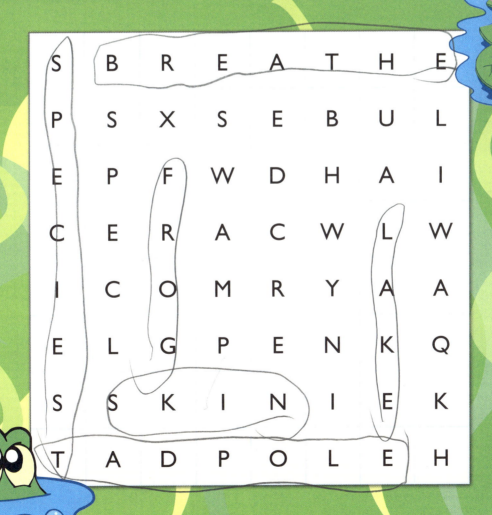

S	B	R	E	A	T	H	E
P	S	X	S	E	B	U	L
E	P	F	W	D	H	A	I
C	E	R	A	C	W	L	W
I	C	O	M	R	Y	A	A
E	L	G	P	E	N	K	Q
S	S	K	I	N	I	E	K
T	A	D	P	O	L	E	H

Beastly biters

Alligators, crocodiles, and the Indian gharial have lots of scary teeth. They grow new teeth if any are broken.

Alligators

There are two species of alligator—the huge American alligator and the much smaller Chinese alligator. Alligators live in swamps, ponds, rivers, and **wetlands.** They eat other reptiles, **mammals,** and birds.

▼ An alligator kills its prey, such as this brown pelican, by gripping it and pulling it underwater.

▲ The male gharial has a small lump on the end of its snout. It uses this to to blow bubbles to get the attention of female gharials.

Indian gharial

The Indian gharial lives in the rivers of India, Bangladesh, Nepal, and Bhutan. Males can reach almost 20 feet (6 meters) long. The gharial is very quick in the water. It catches small fish and other creatures by snapping its jaws as it moves its head from side to side.

Caimans

Caimans are the largest predators in South America's **Amazon basin**. They can reach 13 to 16 feet (4 to 5 meters) long. Caimans eat fish, turtles, birds, deer, and even **anacondas**.

▼ An adult caiman can swallow prey, such as large fish, whole.

89

How long?

Crocodiles and alligators come in many different sizes. Color the creature below that is the longest and the one that is the shortest.

How big?

Use the greater than > or less than < to show which animal is bigger. The first one has been done for you.

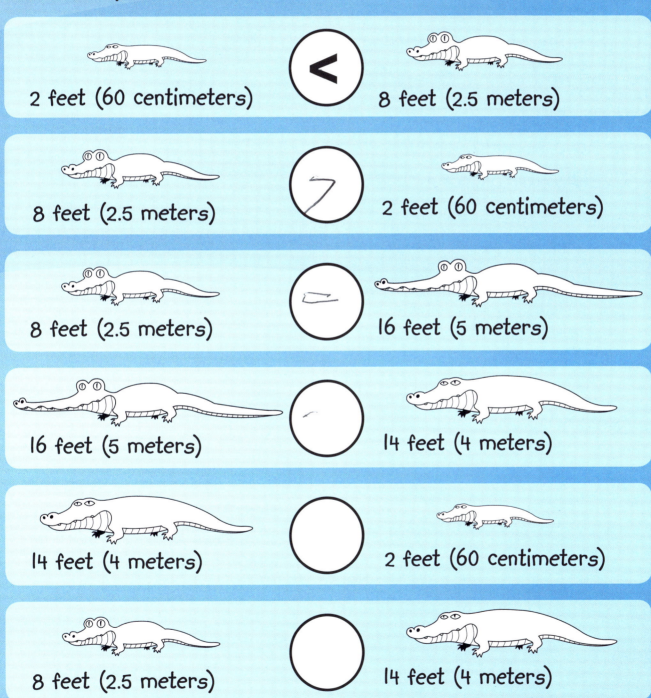

2 feet (60 centimeters)   <   8 feet (2.5 meters)

8 feet (2.5 meters)   >   2 feet (60 centimeters)

8 feet (2.5 meters)   <   16 feet (5 meters)

16 feet (5 meters)   14 feet (4 meters)

14 feet (4 meters)   2 feet (60 centimeters)

8 feet (2.5 meters)   14 feet (4 meters)

Tricky tongues

Foul fact!

The fangs of the diamondback rattlesnake can be more than 1 inch (2.5 centimeters) long.

The tongues of some reptiles are long and sticky. Some have tongues that are V-shaped, and some have colored tongues that they stick out to scare away predators.

▼ A Parson's chameleon can catch prey up to one-and-a-half times its body length away.

Chameleons

When a chameleon sees prey, such as a grasshopper, it sticks out its tongue. As the chameleon's tongue hits the prey, it makes a cup shape that sticks to the prey and stops it from getting away. The chameleon then pulls the prey back into its mouth.

Diamondback rattlesnakes

The two species of diamondback rattlesnake are North America's most poisonous snakes. They scare away predators by shaking the rattle at the end of their tail.

▲ The diamondback rattlesnake has a large, forked tongue.

Blue-tongued skinks

Blue-tongued skinks live in Australia and New Guinea. They sleep in leaf litter or fallen logs, and during the day hunt for snails, slugs, insects, spiders, berries, flowers, fungi, and carrion.

▶ The blue-tongued skink sticks out its blue tongue to scare away predators.

Rattlesnake riddle

Label the rattlesnake below with the right word. Use the word bank to help you.

head	tongue
rattle	skin

Salamander supper

Color the things below that a salamander eats.

carrot

cucumber

lizard

praying mantis

grasshopper

hamburger

bird

95

Spooky spiders

Spiders can move very fast. Some spiders jump out and surprise their prey. Others inject poison when they bite.

▲ A funnel web spider sits at the entrance to its burrow, ready to pounce on its prey.

Tarantulas
There are 800 to 1,000 species of tarantulas living in the world. Some live in deserts, others live rain forests. They eat insects, other spiders, small **reptiles**, frogs, and even small birds.

Funnel web spiders
Funnel web spiders live in Australia. They have sharp **fangs** that they use to inject **venom** into their prey. Their bites can kill humans.

◄ Although tarantulas are venomous, no one is known to have died from a tarantula bite.

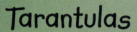

▼ The webs of golden orb web spiders are strong enough to catch birds, although the spiders do not eat them.

Golden orb web spiders

Golden orb web spiders live in Africa and Australia. The spiders are small, but their webs can be up to 6.5 feet (2 meters) wide. The silk is so strong that some people have used the webs to cover cuts and stop them bleeding.

Foul fact!

"Golden" in the golden orb web spider's name describes the color of the web.

SPOT THE SPIDER

Who's in the web?

Here is a spider web. Draw your own spooky spider in the center of the web.

Spider puzzle

Where do the missing pieces go?

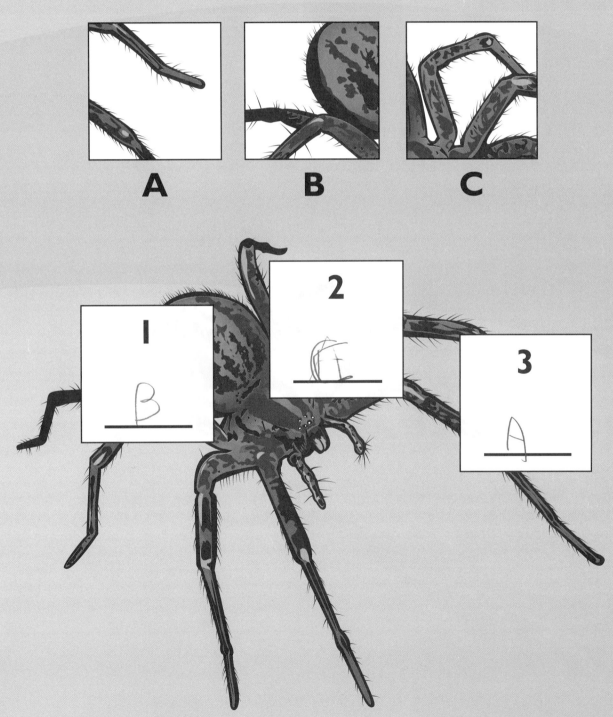

A

B

C

1

B

2

3

A

Foul flies

Flies can be very annoying, buzzing around and landing on food. If you take a closer look, they are amazing flyers.

▲ Blowflies include greenbottles and bluebottles.

Snakeflies

There are about 200 different snakefly species. Snakeflies eat aphids and young caterpillars. The female lays her eggs under the bark of trees. The eggs hatch into **larvae** that live under bark and in **leaf litter**.

▼ An adult snakefly can lift its head high above the rest of its body.

Blowflies

Female blowflies lay eggs on meat or on the wounds, or cuts, of animals. A female blowfly can lay up to 2,000 eggs in her life. Only eight hours after being laid, the eggs hatch into maggots.

Foul fact!

Snakeflies are one of only two insects that can run backward.

Robber flies

Robber flies are often found in dry, sandy places. They eat spiders, beetles, other flies, butterflies, bees, and other flying insects. A robber fly catches its prey in the air. It has a sharp point on its head that it sticks into its prey. Then it injects **saliva** into it. The saliva paralyzes the prey, so that the robber fly can suck out its juices.

▶ A robber fly has a thick, bristly moustache that helps protect its face from prey trying to escape.

COUNT IT!

All about flies

How many snakeflies are underneath the first magnifying glass?

How many blowflies are underneath the second magnifying glass?

How many robber flies are under the third magnifying glass?

How many flies are there all together?

Legs aplenty

Each of these different kinds of fly have 6 legs.
How many do all of the flies have in total?

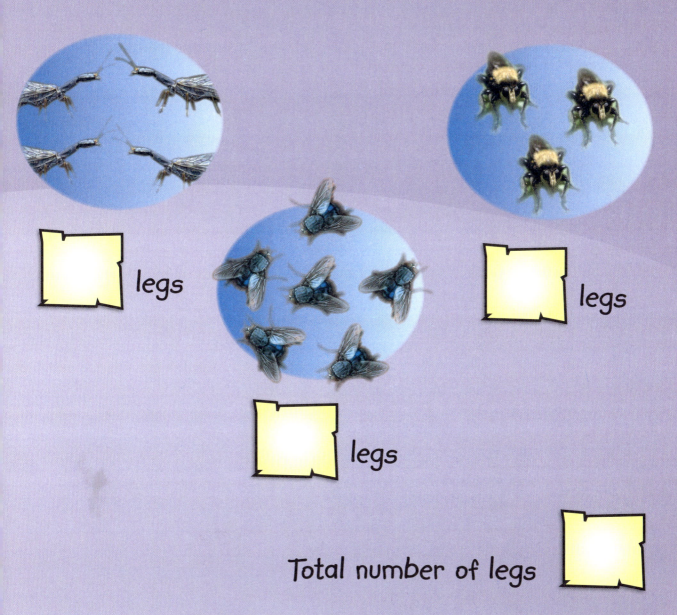

legs

legs

legs

Total number of legs

Nasty nippers

Some creepy crawlers have pincers at their tail end. In some species these are harmless, but in others they can give a nasty nip.

Hellgrammites

Hellgrammites are the larvae of dobsonflies. They hide under rocks in streams and wait for prey to pass. When the larvae are 2 to 3 years old, they burrow into soil. Two weeks later, they become adult dobsonflies, and only live for two more weeks.

Earwigs

There are about 1,800 species of earwigs. During the day, they hide in dark cracks and under stones. At night, they hunt for other insects, plants, and fruit. Some earwigs use their nippers to hold on to prey.

◀ Fishermen sometimes use hellgrammites as bait.

Long ago, people believed that earwigs crawled inside the ears of people as they slept.

▲ Earwigs can open and close their nippers like scissors.

Diplurans

Diplurans look like tiny, pale earwigs. They have pincers at their tail end. To catch prey, a dipluran hides in soil until only its pincers are above ground. If tiny creatures pass by, the dipluran snatches them into the burrow it has made in the soil and eats them.

▶ Diplurans do not have eyes. Instead they can sense where light is to find their way around.

WING WONDER

WARNING

How do insects fly?

Find out how insects' wings work in this fun experiment.

You will need:

- Ruler
- Scissors
- Tissue paper

1. Cut a 1 inch (2.5 centimeters) by 8 inches (20 centimeters) piece of tissue paper.

2. Hold the strip of paper below your bottom lip against your chin.

3. Blow hard on the strip of
   paper. What happens to it?
   It should move
   upward.

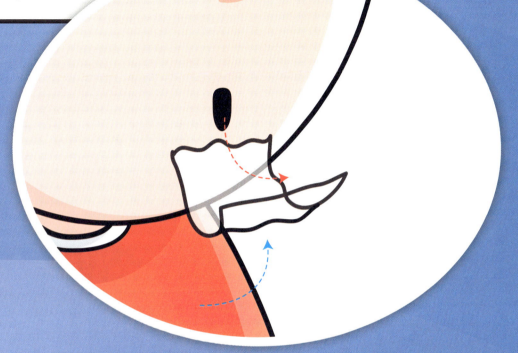

What happened?

When you blow on the top of the strip, you create
a stream of air that moves faster than the air
below the strip. When an insect flies, the wings
of the insect pull air from above the insect that
moves faster than the air below it. This makes the
the insect move forward, just like the tissue paper.

Beastly beetles

The ancient Egyptians believed that scarabs, or dung beetles, kept the world revolving like a huge ball of dung. They carved statues of them in some of their temples.

Dung beetles

Dung beetles live in many different habitats, including deserts and forests. They eat the dung, or poop, of plant-eating animals, such as rabbits, cattle, and elephants.

▼ Some dung beetles roll animal dung into balls larger than themselves.

Burying beetles

Burying beetles bury dead creatures, such as birds or mice, in a hole in the soil. They use the feathers or fur from the animal and line the hole with it. The female lays her eggs in the soil around the hole. When the eggs hatch, the larvae eat the dead body.

◄ Burying beetles can detect dead animals, such as this slug, from a long way off.

Stag beetles

Stag beetle larvae live for many years, eating rotting wood. They can be found in the woodlands and in parks and gardens that have tree stumps or logs. The larvae change, or **metamorphose**, into beetles in summer.

Foul fact!

Some burying beetles regurgitate the flesh of dead animals to feed their babies.

► Male stag beetles have big jaws that look like antlers. They use them to fight each other.

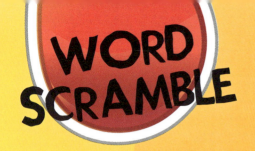

WORD SCRAMBLE

Beastly beetles

Fill in the missing letters about beetles.
Use the letter bank to help you.

e   s   t   d   g

beetl ___

desert ___

fores ___

grasslan ___

dun ___

Beetle life

Use verbs to complete the sentences about beetles. Look at the verb bank for some clues.

change   fly   bury   suck   fight

Stag beetles _____ rival males.

Dung beetles _____ liquid out of manure.

Burying beetles _____ dead creatures.

The larvae of stag beetles _____ into beetles.

Stag beetles _____ in search of mates.

Creepy disguise

Many bugs camouflage, or hide, themselves. Some hide from predators, and others hide to catch prey.

▲ The decorator crab camouflages itself all over so that predators find it hard to spot.

▼ The orchid mantis is a type of praying mantis. Its legs look like petals.

Decorator crab

The decorator crab has small hooks on its back. It uses these to attach seaweed to itself. The decorations act as camouflage. Sometimes the crab attaches itself to a sea anemone. Predators, such as octopuses, do not attack them because anemones sting.

Flower mantids

Flower mantids look like the flowers that they live on. Their camouflage helps them to hide from predators and to catch prey. The mantids sit very still and wait for prey, such as flies, to come close to them. Then they pounce.

The female Macleay's specter stick insect can curl her tail over her body like a scorpion.

▶ If threatened, the Macleay's specter stick insect sways like a leaf in the wind.

Macleay's specter stick insect

The Macleay's specter stick insect, or giant prickly stick insect, lives in New Guinea and northern Australia. A female can lay thousands of eggs in her lifetime. The eggs can take up to two years to hatch.

MAZE MUDDLE

Spot the stick insects

Where is the stick insect? Circle five stick insects in the scene below.

Mantid maze

Help the flower mantid get through the maze and back to its home.

Glossary

Amazon basin
The Amazon basin is the part of South America drained by the Amazon River.

Amphibians
Animals that can live both on land and in water, such as frogs, toads, newts, and salamanders.

Anacondas
Anacondas are large snakes that kill prey animals by crushing them with their body.

Bacteria
Very tiny organisms that can cause disease.

Barbel
A barbel is a whisker found on the heads of some fish. Barbels are used as feelers. Some fish use them to find prey.

Camouflage
An animal that is camouflaged is difficult to spot because its patterns or colors blend in with the background.

Carrion
The dead or decaying flesh of an animal.

Den
Some wild animals make a den or lair in which to sleep, rest or hibernate. They may use a natural hollow in the ground, or may build a den using leaves and branches.

Endangered
In danger of dying out or becoming extinct.

Extinct
If a species is extinct, it has died out—none of its kind are living.

Feces
Waste matter that passes out from an animal's anus.

Fangs
Long, sharp teeth. A snake's fangs are often hollow and are used to inject venom into their prey.

Fungi
Plants without leaves or flowers, such as yeasts, molds, mushrooms, and toadstools.

Gills

The gills of a fish are the parts of its body that extract oxygen from water, allowing the fish to breathe. They are usually found behind the head of a fish.

Gland

A specific part of an animal's body that secretes substances.

Habitat

The natural surroundings of an animal.

Larva

The young of any invertebrate – an animal without a backbone, such as an insect. A larva is also the young of an animal that changes its form. A tadpole, for example, is the larva of a frog. Larvae hatch from eggs.

Leaf litter

Dead plant material made from decaying leaves, twigs, and bark.

Mammal

Mammals are warm-blooded animals with backbones and hair. They produce live young, not eggs. There are around 5,400 species of mammals, ranging from the huge blue whale to the tiny bumblebee bat.

Metamorphose

When an animal goes through metamorphosis, it changes completely. A caterpillar changes into a butterfly or moth, and a tadpole changes into a frog.

Nectar

Nectar is a sugary liquid produced by plants. Some birds, such as hummingbirds, drink nectar. As they do so, they pollinate the plants that make the nectar, and this enables the plants to produce new seeds.

Nymphs

The young or larval stage of some animals. Nymphs change into a different form as they become adults.

Predator

A creature that hunts and kills other animals for food.

Prey

An animal that is hunted by another animal.

Reptile

Cold-blooded animals that have a backbone and short legs or no legs at all, such as snakes, lizards, and crocodiles.

Saliva

The liquid produced in the mouth to keep it moist and to help break down and swallow food.

Scavenger

A scavenger hunts for and eats dead animals, or carrion. Vultures and hyenas are scavengers.

Snout

The projecting nose and mouth of an animal.

Species

A group of animals that shares characteristics. Animals of the same species can breed with each other.

Spur

A sharp, bony spike on the back of an animal's leg.

Suction

The act of sucking. Some animals have suction cups on their feet or legs that help them to grip their prey or slippery, steep surfaces.

Tadpoles

The newly hatched young of creatures such as frogs, toads and newts.

Termite mound

Termites construct a nest about one metre below the ground. Above the nest, they pile up the earth into huge mounds full of tunnels, where they live.

Toxins

A toxin is a poisonous substance, especially one that is produced by bacteria. The saliva produced by the Komodo dragon is a toxin.

Tropical

Tropical relates to the tropics – the area on either side of the equator. The tropics are usually hot and damp.

Venom

Venom is the poison used by some mammals, snakes and spiders to paralyze or kill their prey.

Venomous

A venomous creature uses poison to paralyze or kill its prey.

Wetlands

Wetlands are naturally wet areas, such as marshes or swamps. They have spongy soil.

Zooplankton

Animal plankton, made up of small crustaceans and fish larvae.

Index

Index

Answers

p.11   The Antarctic starfish can have
       up to 50 arms.

p.19   Platypus are different to other
       mammals because they lay eggs
       instead of giving birth to babies.

p.66   Earthworms have up to
       five hearts.

p.83   Poison dart frogs live in the trees
       of rain forests.

p.87   There are about 5,000 species,
       or kinds, of frog.